Food for thought
100 poems that make you think.

Zack Ripley

Copyright 2020

All rights reserved,

including the right to reproduce this book or its contents in any form.

For questions, comments, concerns, address the publisher at smalltownpoetry@aol.com.

Introduction

For those unfamiliar with the phrase, food for thought means something that makes you think. So, with that, I have picked 100 of my most meaningful and thought-provoking poems, categorized alphabetically.

These poems are completely fictional, and cover a variety of topics, including some potentially sensitive ones such as drunk driving and homelessness. I have included these in hopes that they will inspire conversations. I hope you enjoy my work.

My previous book, Out of the darkness into the light, available on amazon, I donated two dollars from every sale to the Jed Foundation. This time, I am donating 100% of profits, 6 dollars from every book to the national coalition for homeless veterans. Thank you for your help in supporting these amazing organizations.

Special thanks

Once again, thank you mom and dad for your encouragement and believing in me.

Thank you to everyone who bought my first book.

Thank you, Faye, for letting me write my poems on the clock □.

Thank you to all my fans (Aleah, Charlene, Ciec, Courtney, Frank, Jessie, John, Karen, Mrs. Countryman, Yasin, my hello poetry fans.)

Thank you, Scott and Justin, for being the first people outside my family and family friends who accepted me and encouraged me. You're a big part of the reason I'm the man I am today.

Thank you, World Poetry Open Mic family, for helping me gain my confidence as a writer.

Thank you, Dawn, for letting me sell my books in your boutique shop, simply positive.

Thank you, Michael, for all you've done and will continue to do.

Thank you, Joey, for your suggestions.

And of course, thank you, Kelly, for being my inspiration to keep going.

Table of contents

61. New skin
62. Night doesn't last forever
63. No one, everyone, anyone, someone
64. Not alone
65. Not the end
66. Not your job
67. Once upon a time
68. One more
69. One-way ticket
70. Only time will tell
71. Protect yourself
72. Questions and answers
73. Rainbow within you
74. Real
75. Reflection from our imperfections
76. Roar
77. Room
78. Say it
79. Second chances
80. See you at the end
81. Stick together
82. Still a good day
83. Stuck in the middle
84. Support
85. Tell me
86. Tell your story
87. That's what it's all about
88. The games of life and love
89. The more you know
90. These days

10 miles from home

When she goes out, it's like it's her last night alive.
When he goes out, he likes to clear his mind
By taking a midnight drive through the countryside.
After a long night alone in an empty bar,
She decided to take a chance and get in her car.
He went out too but didn't make it very far.
Only ten miles.
Ten miles from home, two lives were lost.
Ten miles from home, she didn't think about the cost.
Ten miles from home, a memorial lies
With their pictures and names.
Ten miles from home, two families will never be the same.

About this poem

Ten miles from home is a poem about drunk driving. The title was inspired by a statistic that says over 70 percent of accidents happen within ten miles from the driver's home.

While completely fictional and not based on any real events, drunk driving is a very real thing. With resources ranging from Turbo Taxi to designated drivers, please don't take a chance. Be safe.

Accept, reject, believe

I accept there will be times when we don't see eye to eye.
After all, you grew up different than I.
I accept that someday, place and time, we will die.
I accept the idea that we have souls.
That there are things that can happen
That are out of our control.
But I reject the suggestion
That there's nothing we can do to change it.
I reject that everything is black and white. Wrong or right.
I reject that life is a one-way street.
Because I believe in second chances.
That there are more than two ways of looking at things.
And most importantly, I believe that even if you go down
One path, eventually, you can choose a different one.
I know that what I accept, reject, and believe
Isn't necessarily relevant to you.
But different perspectives can help you get through.

About this poem

Accept, reject, believe was an exercise to look inside
myself and think about how I view things like death,
fate/destiny. Concepts that are subject to controversy or
denial. But it's also about inspiring others to look at these
things in a different way.

Almost

Almost out of energy.
Almost out of time.
Almost out of patience.
Almost out of rhymes.
Almost out of love.
Almost out of space.
Almost ready to give up and leave this wretched place.
But every time I feel I'm ready to say goodbye,
I think about all the people I'd have to leave behind.
I think about all the memories that would be erased.
Some good. Others bad.
I think about all the adventures I'd never get to have.
Life can be exhausting. Painful.
So, I can understand why you'd want it to end.
But take it from me.
You never know what you'll miss.
You never know who will miss you.
And you never know
What's just around the river bend.

About this poem

You'll hear me talk about my mental health in this book.
There was a time when I was bullied so bad, I felt so
worthless, a burden, I was prepared to end my life. But I
knew I had people who loved me and that it would hurt
them. That they would blame themselves. But then I saw
the other side of the river bend. I became friends with
someone in animal science. Everything changed.

Ask the right question

"What are you doing to better the world?"
"What value do you bring to society?"
"Those are not the right questions."
"Why not? They're questions everyone asks."
"Maybe so. But they're meaningless
If you can't answer another one first."
"Which is?"
"The right question is
"What are you doing to better yourself?"
If you can't find value in yourself,
If you don't think you're the best you can be,
You can't be ready to better the world.

About this poem

Whether it's for an interview or just brought up in a
conversation between people, one question that always
seems to be brought up in some way is how you can add
value. Sure, it's a good way to gauge how much
confidence and self-esteem you have for yourself. But the
more important question is, what are you doing to take
care of yourself?

Be afraid

Don't be afraid to fall in love.
Don't be afraid to have your heart break.
Don't be afraid to start over.
Don't be afraid to do whatever it takes.
Don't be afraid that he's the one.
Don't be afraid if she makes your heart run.
Don't be afraid of what your family will think.
Don't be afraid that you're too young.
Why shouldn't you be afraid?
Because love is worth living for.
Because if your heart breaks,
When someone helps heal it,
It's going to mean that much more.
Because you never know what life has in store.
Because we all have the right to pursue happiness.
Because it starts with one.
Because whatever or whoever makes you happy
Is your business and yours alone.
Because even if it doesn't work,
Trying is the only way to grow.

About this poem

At this point, you all know how important I think love is in
life. This poem looks at the things people fear about love,
like falling too fast, being too young for it, heartbreak, that
people will treat you differently if you are with someone,
and suggests that those fears shouldn't stop you from
doing it.

Beautiful, fallible humans

Yes, we are part of the United States of America.
And yes, it is important to be proud
Of where you live and come from.
But it doesn't matter how united we are.
We will always be divided some way.
But that's okay. Because we still work together.
We're still human.
I know you're probably sick of me saying that word.
But the fact is, we can't be proud
Of where we live, where we come from.
We can't make social change
Until we're proud to be what we are.
Beautiful, fallible humans.

About this poem

Pride. We have a lot of it for a few things. One of them
being pride about where we live and come from. But that
pride can only mean so much if you're not proud of who
you are.
This poem suggests that it can be more inspiring to people
if you're proud of the fact and accept the fact that you're
fallible and you're human.

Believe

I want to thank you
For letting me see the wonder in your eyes.
The ones that shine brighter than the stars in the sky.
I want to thank you for making me believe
That it's okay for me to chase my dreams.
All the times I thought I lost my way,
I prayed for guidance, and I swear I heard you say:
It's okay if you feel lost.
It's okay if you don't know which way to go.
Don't be afraid of taking chances.
Sometimes that's the only way to know.
But if you're afraid, just listen to your heart.
You can always find your way back home.

About this poem

Believe is the first part of an original, full length song that I
wrote after watching the movie I still believe. At the heart of
it, the poem is about having faith, believing in something,
and having the courage to take chances. If you would like
to listen to me singing the full song, look up small town
poetry on Youtube.

Best I can do is hope

I don't understand. I know I'll never understand.
I just wish you would have reached out for my hand.
I would have raised you up. Got you back on your feet.
Help you realize life doesn't have to be a one-way street.
But there's nothing I can say.
No, there's nothing I can do to bring you back.
So, I'll just remember you and hope.
Hope you're in a better place
Where the sunshine kisses on your face.
I hope the beer tastes better
And that it's always perfect hunting and fishing weather.
I hope you remember us. And know that we'll remember you.
It'll be hard to push through, but we'll find a way to cope.
But until we meet again, the best I can do is hope.
Ever since the day you left,
my heart feels like it's been a victim of theft.
And every time I see your face in a photograph,
I can't help but sit back and laugh.
Then, your voice pops in my head.
And I remember all the things left unsaid.
I wasn't ready to let you go, but I need you to know.
I forgive you. And hope you're in a better place
Where the sunshine kisses on your face.
I hope the beer tastes better,
And that it's always perfect hunting and fishing weather.
I hope you remember us. And know that we'll remember you.
It'll be hard to push through, but we'll find a way to cope.
But until we meet again, the best I can do is hope.
You taught me how to be a better man.
And you showed me how to be a better friend.
And these are lessons I'll take with me to the end.
But there's nothing I can say. No, there's nothing I can do
To bring you back. So, I'll just remember you and hope.
The best I can do is hope.

About this poem

This is a song I wrote when a family friend committed suicide. I
hope it helps anyone who's lost someone, whatever the
circumstance. Roger, this is for you.

Better days

First thing you see on the evening news,
Mama cries in a sea of camera crews.
She pleas for justice, but we just stop and stare.
We could do so much better if we tried to care.
Mama's back to work after a week to grieve.
She can't help but wear her broken heart on her sleeve.
She breaks down and says "I need more time."
Boss says "sorry. There's the unemployment line."
We don't need to change the world.
We just need to change our minds.
We'll see things in a different light
When we pull back the curtains and blinds.
If we remember how to listen to what people say,
Maybe we can find our way back to better days.

About this poem

Better days is about how tragedies, like a local mother
losing her child, are focal points for news reporters but,
after a few days, no one thinks about it anymore because
there's a new story.

The problem with this is people only see the ten minutes
they get to tell their story. They don't usually think about
what happens after.

This poem suggests that if we could look past the tragedy,
if we could focus on her asking for help, we might get back
to a time where we didn't feel so isolated. So alone. A time
when people had better mental health.

Be whoever you want to be

If you could live forever, would you ever
Let anyone stop you from chasing your dreams?
Dreams to be a singer, to do something that matters,
Have all the money and material things?
I know that's not something we can do,
But if that doesn't matter to you:
If you can handle the bad times,
If you can handle the cold nights,
If you're willing to do whatever it takes.
If you're okay being lonely,
Then you're the only one who can stand in your way.
If you don't let time be your enemy,
You can be whoever you want to be.

About this poem

At some point, you, or someone you know has said "I don't
have enough time to do that." This poem reminds that
there are sacrifices required to make your dreams come
true. But if you're willing to put in the work, and sacrifice
comfort and happiness for a while, it doesn't matter how
much or little time you have or how young or old you are.
You can be whoever you want to be.

Be you

For years, you've asked questions
You can never seem to find the answer to.
"How do I make someone love me?"
"How do I know if my feelings are true?"
So tonight, I have a secret I'd like to share with you.
It's something not a lot of people know how to do.
The secret? Be you.
I know vulnerability is scary.
But true love gets its strength from the heart.
And if you can find the courage
To be proud of who you are,
You may not find love immediately,
But it's a good place to start.

About this poem

There's a famous phrase that goes "you can't love
someone until you love yourself." At least from my
experience, the difficult part about loving yourself is that it
can make you feel vulnerable. But vulnerability is not
something that should be feared when it comes to love.

This poem is a challenge to not be afraid of hiding who you
are.

Brave

The air should be light.
Filled with joy, not fright.
On this cold winter night.
And for most, it is.
The difference between them and me, you see,
Is that they are not prisoners of their minds. They are free.
I was sentenced to this life alone
Without a home to call my own,
After I served my country.
Oh, what a world I was shown.
Don't misunderstand. I had a good life.
I lived the American dream.
Complete with a house, a dog, a beautiful wife.
But once I signed up for another tour,
Her heart couldn't take it anymore.
She walked out the door.
When I came back, I was too ashamed to ask for help.
So that's how I got here,
Feeling like I only have myself to blame.
But even as I join my fellow outcasts,
Forgotten, and unloved,
I smile with pride knowing I was brave enough
To play the game.

About this poem

When I saw a prompt to write a poem about the outcasts,
forgotten, and unloved of society, I thought the homeless might
feel this way. This is a story of how a veteran became homeless,
based on research that suggests "the greatest risk factors for
homelessness are lack of support and social isolation after
discharge." (Taken from an article about homeless veteran facts
from greendoors.org) If you are homeless and are reading this,
and you feel unloved, I hope you believe me when I say that
even if you don't know it, there are people who love you. I hope
you understand it's ok to ask for help. And most importantly, I
hope that you do feel brave and know you're appreciated.

Broken home

When I left home, I was broken and bruised.
Daddy took it out on me when he fell victim to the booze.
I thought when I graduated, I'd finally get to choose.
Find a world where bars played rock instead of the blues.
The day everything changed, there was a fork in the road.
There was a wise old man, and this is what I was told.
"If you go to the left, you'll stay in hell.
But you'll get your revenge when he dies in a cell.
But if you don't want revenge, go to the right.
You'll travel the world. You'll make a difference.
But it will be hard to sleep at night."
I didn't have to think. I ran to the right.
He told me it would never be the same
If I ever had to come back.
But I was okay with that.
I had everything I needed in my sack.
Five years later, I woke up alone in bed.
A purple heart hung above my head.
Even though I am where I am today, I don't regret it.
Because I know that when I go to my grave,
And someone is asked to describe me,
They'll say "he was brave."

About this poem

After I finished writing brave, Nick suggested I write it from
the perspective of someone going into the military because
they come from an abusive home. So, because everyone
has a different story, I wrote broken home. Again, if you're
reading this, it's okay to ask for help. You are brave. And
you are appreciated and loved.

Did you know?

Did you know someone's proud of you?
That someone finds you beautiful inside and out?
Did you know someone loves you for who you are?
That you don't have to feel ashamed of your scars?
Did you know that you're enough? That you're strong?
Even through the computer, I can see you crying,
Saying "you're wrong."
But I'm telling you these things because they're true.
Even if they're not true now, they will be.
Now say it with me.
"Someone's proud of me."
"Someone finds me beautiful, inside and out."
"Someone loves me for who I am."
"I don't have to be ashamed of my scars."
"I'm enough. I'm strong."
One more thing. "It's okay to tell my story."

About this poem

In my last book, I said that doubts are the bullies of the
mind. Doubt goes hand in hand with self-esteem issues.
It's hard for people to believe when someone says
something positive about them because they can't see it in
themselves.
But if you say something enough, you start to believe it.
So, this poem challenges you to say these things in hopes
that once you start to believe them, you'll start to feel
better. Confident. Worthy.

Don't

Stop! PLEASE stop saying "don't."
"Don't give up."
"Don't be afraid to ask for help."
"Don't be sad."
"Don't keep it bottled up inside."
I could go on and on.
"Don't be scared."
God, I hate that one the most.
Like, why the hell shouldn't I be scared?
Look at everything that's happening.
Look, I know you mean well,
But when you say that word,
It feels like you're trying to control me.
And I already feel
                    So
                    Out
                    Of
                    Control.
I know you want to help.
And it means a lot to know you'll be there if I need help.
But I need to do this on my own.

About this poem

I know this poem kind of contradicts all the poems that
encourage you to not give up or hide your feelings, but this
is a soliloquy; a conversation someone has with
themselves. Once again, perspective. This poem looks into
the mind of someone who prefers to be a loner and doesn't
want people worrying about them just because they're
alone.

Don't say sorry

Didn't see the signs
Or read between the lines.
Was blind because you were mine.
Didn't take the time
To make sure you were the one for me.
Just didn't want to be lonely.
And now you're going to leave me anyway.
But when you do,
Don't say "sorry, it's the way it has to be."
Don't say "sorry. Maybe we're not meant to be."
If you want to leave, I won't make you stay.
But if you want to leave, I promise I'll be okay.

About this poem

When I was younger, the only thing I wanted was to be in a relationship. It always made me upset when people said that relationships were over-rated. They always said never settle.

The fact is, I would have settled in a heartbeat just to know what it felt like to have someone to come home to. This poem is about me trying to understand how it might not be worth it to be in a relationship.

Telling myself that if someone I was in a relationship with wanted to end it, or if the relationship was toxic, I would be okay if I had to be lonely again.

Don't walk away angry

Today, I found you crying on the stairs.
I asked if you were okay.
You asked me why I cared. So I sat down beside you.
I said "I know you didn't ask for one,
but you look like you could use a friend."
I asked again "what's wrong? Are you okay?"
You said "I'm fine. Just go away!"
I looked in your eyes and only saw pain and fear.
So I said "we don't have to talk. But I'm not going anywhere."
You groaned and put your head in your knees.
Finally, you looked up and said "want to know what happened? Fine!
I found out my boyfriend cheated on me.
When I confronted him, he said he never loved me
And I needed to leave. Is that what you want to hear?!"
"No. I'm sorry that happened.
Do you have any friends or family near?"
"No. And I don't have any money either."
"Alright. Before you say it,
I know you have no reason to trust me.
But if you want, you can stay with me."
"Why are you being so nice to me? Why do you care?"
"Years ago, I had a friend who had gone through
A traumatic experience and I wanted to help her.
I thought she could heal if she talked to me about it.
I pushed her too hard and she yelled at me. So I yelled back.
I was angry, so I left and ignored her pleas to come back.
Found out later she killed herself.
I don't know if anything would have changed if I stayed.
But I wish I didn't get angry and walk away."

About this poem

Fictional poem. It's about how you never want the last thing you
say to someone you love or care about be said in anger.

Do whatever it takes

Hiding how you feel isn't lying.
In fact, for some people, it's a form of surviving.
It may not be the healthiest way to heal;
Ignoring the pain and feelings to the point It's not real.
But do whatever it takes to see tomorrow.

About this poem

Internalizing your fears and feelings is not exactly safe for
your mental health. But some things can be too painful to
talk about. Especially because saying something out loud
makes it real.
The point of this poem is that everyone has a different way
of processing things. And as long as you keep going, don't
worry about what anyone else thinks. Do whatever it takes.

Down

Going down, but it's not bad.
Going down to the river to clear my head.
Simple things like skipping rocks
Or catching fish in the stream
Remind me that even in times like these,
Life could still be a dream.

About this poem

Everyone needs an escape. Now more than ever. Down is
about finding something that relaxes you and reminds you
that there are still good things in bad times.

Emotion

Everyone fell in love with your beauty and grace.
But no one saw the tears that streamed down your face.
Because people only see what they want to see.
"If that's true," you ask,
"Does that mean you wanted to see me cry?"
"Not at all, my dear. I just think emotion is beautiful.
And when you are willing to show an emotion like crying,
It proves there's more to you than meets the eye."

About this poem

Another recurring theme, this is another poem about
vulnerability. But it's also a commentary, an observation,
on how we deal things we are uncomfortable with. Like
seeing someone cry.
Don't be afraid to talk about or show how you're feeling.
Being open about how you feel shouldn't be embarrassing.
It's brave. It's sexy. It proves you're willing to put all you
have in a relationship.

End of the line

You made me play your game. Now I'll never be the same.
I believed the lie you told.
Now that I know the truth, I've never felt so cold. So alone.
Heart feels heavy like it's made of stone.
I can feel myself sinking.
Ever closer to depression. Despair.
In desperation I cry out "is anyone there?"
No one answers of course.
Then your voice pops in my head, saying "nobody cares."
For a second, I believe it.
Then I remember your deceit. In a moment of clarity,
I realize listening to you would mean I admit defeat.
But I won't let you win.
I'll take your words and make them mine.
It's the end of the line.

About this poem

End of the line is about being manipulated by someone,
and how it feels when they realize they were being fooled.
The frustration that they weren't able to figure it out. But it's
also about moving on. Taking the power back for yourself.

Enough

Life is full of ups and downs.
But we've been down so long,
I can't help but wonder, when the time comes,
Can we even remember HOW to get up?
And when will that time come?
When someone has the courage to scream one word.
ENOUGH!
Enough kneeling.
It's time to stand and start healing.
But it's all or no one. So...
Have you had enough?"

About this poem

2020 was a bad year for us. We had been feeling down for
so long, I wondered what it would take for us to all get back
to normal again. And I realized it starts with one.
It just takes one person to say "enough." But it can't finish
with just one. Everyone needs to do their part.

Erase

Sometimes, I wish my story
Was written with a pencil instead of a pen.
To be able to erase all the bad times,
The mistakes, The what could've been's.
But in the end, I wouldn't trade them for anything.
They made me who I am today.
And to me, that's everything.

About this poem

Erase is about wishing that you could take back things you
said or wish that you did differently. That decisions we
make aren't permanent. But honestly, we learn by doing
things wrong. And it's learning from mistakes that help
make you into a better, more informed person. John, this
poem's for you.

Everyone is someone

Everyone is someone in some way, shape, or form.
And everyone has been through hell
Or survived a storm.
Some made it out better than others.
Some didn't make it out at all.
Some were thanked for their bravery
By having their names immortalized on walls.
But even if their names aren't on display
For the world to see,
Everyone has someone live in their hearts.
Even you and me.

About this poem

This poem is about bringing awareness to the fact that
everyone has been through hard and devastating times in
their lives. And even if people have a more difficult time
healing or dealing with it, it doesn't make them any less of
a person or their experience any less devastating.

Fear vs hope

Hope is a horrible thing to be without.
Without it, we would surely drown in doubt.
A lot of people say they feel hopeless.
Here's the thing: the definition of hope is a desire for,
or an expectation for something to happen.
Based on that definition, it's impossible to be without hope.
So, if hope never died, never left, where did it go?
What if your fear that nothing would change or get better
Overpowered your hope that things would change
or get better? How do you get it back?
First, you tell fear you're not afraid anymore.
Then, you show it the door.

About this poem:

This poem was inspired by a line in a book called Game
Changer by Neal Shusterman. "I'd rather live in a world
where hope was alive but sick, than a world where it's
already in the morgue."

Feelings

Good. Bad.
Happy. Sad.
Love. Hate.
Lost.
Weak. Strong.
Right. Wrong.
Scared. Prepared.
These words don't define us.
They are feelings.
So please.
Don't be afraid If these words come across your mind.
Don't be afraid to admit that you feel that way.
Like everything else, they will go away in time.

About this poem

Feelings are incredibly important. But they don't define
who we are as people. If I say I'm a sad person, that's not
who I am all the time. That's just how I am for the moment.
No one IS weak. They just feel weak. That being said, it's
important to respect someone if they say feel that way.

For better or worse

I thought we'd be together forever.
But now for worse, or maybe someday, better,
I will let go of my dream I had for you and me
And sign this letter.

About this poem

This poem is about someone signing a divorce letter and
how, at the time, it may hurt, but it might be for the best.

Forgive

First, I forgave the bullies who made me cry.
I didn't know your story. You didn't ask for mine.
Now the hard part.
I forgive myself for the mistakes I've made.
It's been a long, weird game.
But so far, I don't regret the way I've played.

About this poem

Something that can really help you live a full and happy life
is forgiveness. And a great place to start is with people
who were bullies. In my last book, I suggested that just
because someone bullies you, that doesn't mean they
aren't being bullied as well.

So, even if they don't offer an apology, I believe in
forgiving them. Because we really have no idea what
someone else is going through, and we're not necessarily
interested if they are being mean to us.
The next step is a much harder one. Forgiving yourself for
mistakes you've made. It's harder because we are our
biggest critics. "I should have known that. I should have
seen it coming." But the bottom line is, they're mistakes.
And everyone makes them.

Fortune cookie

Live your life.
Because no one can live your life for you.
And when you dream a dream,
Don't abandon it. Embrace it.
Because only you can make your dream come true.

About this poem

Not much to say. I thought it sounded like a fortune cookie.
Now go make that dream come true!

Get away

If I get lost riding a train of thought,
Please don't come looking for me.
I won't want to be found.
And if you see me struggle to swim in a sea of words,
It's okay. Let me drown.
Here and now, I promise I'll come back to you someday.
But for now, I need to get away.

About this poem

This poem was inspired by the phrase "train of thought." I
took the phrase and decided to make someone riding it be
a metaphor for daydreaming. And sometimes, it can be
healthy to daydream. To escape. Get away is simply about
going into your own little world for a little while.

Good man

When I was a kid, I thought I could be superman.
But now that I'm older, I don't know that anyone can.
So, if I can't be superman,
The next best thing I can be is a good man.

About this poem

When kids are young, they look up to superheroes as
people they should aspire to be. This poem is about
realizing that even if you can't be a superhero, you can still
be a good person. And that's still a worthwhile thing to be.

Gray skies

Have you ever wondered why the sky turns gray
When it rains?
Well, in every creature, there is darkness,
And there is light.
And when you start to give up the fight,
The fight for happiness, love, life,
When you start to lose hope,
The darkness starts to bleed into your light. But it's okay.
The color can come back. First, ask to talk to someone.
Ask them to listen.
Then, hold nothing back.
Don't stop until you understand how you feel.
What you want.
Don't worry. It's not selfish to talk about it.
Not to the people who care about you.
It will take time, but if you do this,
Someday, a rainbow will come shining through.

About this poem

Gray skies is an extension of an exercise that was done in middle school where you had to come up with a reason why it rains. What I hope everyone takes away from this is that if you're feeling down, you can feel better again by talking to someone about what's going on in your head.

I know from personal experience, I felt like asking for help to deal with my emotional health issues wasn't right because other people had it worse. But once I did talk about it, it felt like my feelings were validated. That it was okay to feel them. That nothing was wrong with me.

Hands

Washing my hands even though I know
They'll never really be clean.
Too many stains from the blood, sweat and tears
That will never be seen.
My hands may never be completely clean,
But I won't apologize.
I did what I had to to protect, love, and survive.

About this poem

When I first wrote this, I was only focusing on writing a
poem about a topic that was extremely relevant: washing
your hands. It wasn't until I shared it that someone pointed
out to me that it's the story of a soldier.

Head in the clouds

Keeping my head high in the clouds.
Because it's too exhausting being just another face
In a faceless crowd.

About this poem

Head in the clouds is a metaphor for social anxiety. I hear
people say all the time that they feel like they're just
another cog in the machine. Sometimes, it can be
depressing feeling like that; that you blend into the crowd
and don't really know what sets you apart from everyone
else.

Here's to the women

Here's to the women who stay strong.
Here's to the women who got men
To admit they were wrong.
Here's to the women who became mothers.
Here's to the women who don't take crap from others.
Here's to the women who are struggling.
You've got this. This one's for you.
I know we don't say it. So, thank you for everything you do.

About this poem

We don't give enough credit to women and all they do, let
alone respect. So, this poem is dedicated to you, ladies.
Thank you for everything you do and put up with.

How to be successful

"How do I become successful?"
"Are you alive?"
"Yes"
"Then you're already doing it.
Keep it up."

About this poem

Success is subjective. It doesn't have the same meaning
for everyone. So, this poem explores what the basic
requirement to be successful is. You can't be successful if
you aren't alive. And for people struggling with depression,
that alone could be seen as success.

I forgive you

There I was, sound asleep in my bed.
Memories of my wife and I danced in my head.
All of a sudden, I woke up to a chill in the air
And I couldn't help feel like someone was there.
As I laid back down, I heard a knock at the door.
I looked at the clock and it was half past four. (a.m.)
"Who could that be?" I put on my robe,
And as I crept down the hall, I checked in on my daughter.
"Wow. She's not even five and she's already so tall."
The stranger knocked again, so I hurried my pace.
I was about to scream, but then I saw his face.
It was snow. I was so angry, I couldn't speak.
All I could do was glare.
Finally, I said, "what do you think you're doing, standing there?"
"Hey! I just wanted to let you know I was back in town."
He was wearing a smile,
But when he saw I was mad, he replaced it with a frown.
"What's wrong? Aren't you happy to see me?"
I scoffed. "Happy? To see you? You killed my wife!
Last year, she was driving home.
One night, you covered her windshield
And she got into an accident because she couldn't see.
Snow was horrified. He looked me in the eye,
Said "I'm so sorry," and as he walked away, he started to cry.
Just then, my daughter snuck out.
"Snow! Don't go!" I heard her shout.
I couldn't believe it, but she hugged him.
I knelt beside her and asked
"If you know who this man is, why are you happy to see him?"
She said "because even though it's sad she's not here,
Snow was the thing mommy looked forward to the most every
year."
After a moment, I knew what I needed to do.
"Snow, I will never forget what you did
or the pain you put me through.
But in honor of my wife and daughter, I forgive you."

This poem is about seasonal depression, the importance of
forgiveness, and how forgiving children can be. This poem was
so long, I had to make the font smaller for it to fit on one page.

I'll be there for you

Close your eyes. Take a breath.
The pain you feel, the grief,
Won't be the death of you.
Because you've had this pain before.
And even though you're still sore,
There are still people you need to be there for.
Who will be there for you.

About this poem

It's safe to say one of the worst times you will experience
in life is the death of a loved one. This poem is about
having the strength to keep going. Because people will still
look up to you and need you. And they'll be there for you if
you need them.

I'm here to tell you

I've been lost.
I've been found.
I've been up, down, and around.
I've been here.
I've been there.
It feels like I've been everywhere
Without going barely anywhere at all.
I've been accepted.
Rejected.
Made fun of by my peers.
But I'm here to tell you that if I've made it through,
I believe there's hope for you too.
Just breathe, and don't be embarrassed
If you shed a few tears.

About this poem

I won't pretend I have any idea what you've been through.
But I bet I've been in a similar situation before when it
comes to social interactions in high school. I'm here to tell
you is a poem that I hope reassures you that there is hope
even when it doesn't seem like it. If one person can make it
through, if I could make it through, you can too.

I'm still standing

I thought I'd have to go to *another world*
To find *somewhere I belong*.
I felt *powerless*. Alone. A broken man in a *carnival of rust*.
My friends always tried to make me feel *wanted*
By saying "*someone's gonna light you up*."
But I always felt like the only thing people saw
Were my *imperfections*.
They wouldn't have tried so hard to break me
If they saw how good of a person I tried to be, right?
Or is it the opposite?
They didn't want *one more light*
In a world that was already so dark?
Well, they almost won.
I almost tried to see *heaven*.
But *I'm still standing*.
I don't know if it's because I'm a *simple man*
Or because I decided to *stand in the light*,
But I was given a *second chance*.
Now, I *don't worry about a thing*.
Because *what I've got* is all I've ever wanted.
Every time I look in her *angel eyes*,
The black of my *iris* gets lighter.
And now that I see how beautiful life can be,
I'm not afraid to follow you *wherever you will go.*
I'm forever yours, *faithfully*.

About this poem

This poem was a challenge I made myself to write a poem
using the titles of 20 of my favorite songs. It also happens
to be my mom's favorite. So, this one's for you, mom.
Some of the songs are not well known, so if you wanted to
listen to them, I have italicized all the titles. Another world
is by Mackenzie Phillips. The rest you can find by just
entering their names in Youtube.

Is this a change for the good?

Who do you see when you look in the mirror?
Turn away. Now look back.
Is the reflection any clearer?
Does it look the same?
Is it what you thought it'd be?
If it's not, don't worry.
You can change it because you control your destiny.
But just because you can change things
Doesn't necessarily mean you should.
Before you make any decisions,
Ask "is this a change for the good?"

About this poem

I know the wording of the question "is this a change for the good?" is weird. I admit, I wrote it that way because I was going for a rhyme. But the question is still an important one.

It's your body, so if you look in the mirror and are so unhappy about something you see, absolutely go for it. Just make sure you take the time to determine if you're trying to change for the right reasons. Are you changing because you want to change? Or are you trying to change something because someone criticized you and you think it will make them stop?

It's not your fault

It's not your fault if he doesn't say hi as you walk by.
It's not your fault if she doesn't seem to know you exist.
But it's not their fault either.
It's not your fault if you feel too much or nothing at all.
And if it gets bad, there's nothing wrong
With curling up in a ball. We all need an escape.
This is an important one.
It is NOT your fault if you get addicted
To the drugs or the drink.
It's not your fault if you get so stressed,
You can't eat, sleep, or think.
It's not your fault because bad things, confusion,
loneliness, sadness, stress, loss, anger...
It happens to everyone.
It's not a choice.

About this poem

This is probably one of the most important poems in the
book. As I've already talked about before, we are our own
biggest critic. And when we can't find someone else to
blame on something, we end up turning it on ourselves.

This poem is about things we constantly beat ourselves up
for and saying that not everything that happens is
someone's fault.

It's up to you

It's up to you what's wrong or right.
It's up to you whether you want to fight
Or go quietly into the night.
It's up to you whether you want to take this life by the balls
Or fall in line behind the wall.
This is your life. Your body.
You have the power to choose.
Whatever you decide, it's up to you.

About this poem

This poem reminds you that you do have not only the
power, but the right to choose how you live your life.

Just as important

They say "it's not about what you say,
It's about what you do."
But that's not necessarily true.
Like everything, it depends on the situation.
For example, when it came to writing the declaration,
The act of writing it was just as important
As the words they wrote.
What I'm saying is, no one action
Is more important than another.
What we say, what we do, it's all important.
Because in the end, all we have is each other.

About this poem

This poem was written to suggest everything is important
because everything affects us in some way.

Just one

A knife. A gun.
These instruments usually inspire one feeling.
One thought. Fear. Run.
But for some people, it could inspire
A completely different thought. "Just one."
"One slice. One bullet. No more pain.
No more voices in my head driving me insane."
It's amazing.
One is such a small number, but it can change so much.
One slice. One bullet. One kiss. One hug. One touch.
All it takes is one person to say "I love you. I care."
Be that "one."
See how much of a difference you can make
By saying "if you want to talk, I'll be there."

About this poem

One of the most emotional poems I've ever written. It really does take only one thing to make a huge difference. One random encounter outside the public library turned into my first friend. He taught me how to socialize and talk to people.

And then my first and only love changed my whole world. Made me feel like being myself was enough. If you're struggling, please talk to someone.

Know who you are

If you want the world to know who you are,
YOU have to know who you are first.
What you stand for.
What you want to say.
Because one day, they may listen,
But you never know how long they'll stay.

About this poem

This poem is inspired by a scene in A Star Is Born. The
main character tells his love interest that people are
beginning to listen to her. But eventually, they'll stop. So,
while she has their attention, she needs to tell her story,
not apologize for what she has to say, and not worry why
people are listening.

Kung-fu typing

"I wish I could fight."
"You can."
"How? I don't know how to punch or move."
"You fight with words. It's called kung-fu typing."
"Kung-fu typing? Did you just make that up?
Doesn't sound very cool."
"It's not supposed to be. But if you master it,
You'll never need to worry
About not knowing how to punch or move."

About this poem

The literal translation and origin of kung-fu means
"acquired skill." With that in mind, I decided to create a
poem between a kid wishing he were strong and an adult
explaining there are other ways of fighting.

Kung-fu, the martial arts form that we usually associate
with the name, is primarily for self-defense. Which is why I
chose typing. In a world where people are using computers
younger and younger, and being able to hide behind a
keyboard, people are realizing how much words can hurt
people. But you can also use words to defend yourself and
others. This poem suggests that if you can master
choosing your words, that's as effective as knowing how to
defend yourself and others physically.

Last in line

I wanted you to show me the way. To give me a sign.
But I looked behind to realize that, for once,
I wasn't the last one in line.

About this poem

This poem is about someone who has been asking for
guidance for a long time, thinking about himself, only to
look around and realize there were people who needed
guidance and help more than him. You may be struggling,
but a lot of other people are struggling as well.

Let happiness find you

"How are you today?"
"Honestly? Stuck. Frustrated. Like I want to give up."
"Okay. What's making you feel that way?"
"It's been a long time coming.
I feel like I've tried so hard to find happiness.
I'm trying to talk to people.
I'm doing things I love.
But no matter what I do,
I just feel empty. Alone."
"Most of the time, happiness is a watched pot.
It won't happen If you're trying to find it.
Same goes for love.
Let me ask you this. What does happiness mean to you?"
"Uh...I don't know? Hakuna matata?
Being able to actually laugh.
Being able to breathe."
"And can you do that if you spend all your energy
Trying to force that?"
"Okay. I get your point. I'm trying too hard.
So what do I do?"
"Let happiness find you."

About this poem

Let happiness find you is a fictional conversation between
someone and their therapist. I chose to write it this way
because I've done so many preachy poems about finding
self-worth and happiness, I thought it would be more
effective as a conversation, and it seemed like the most
likely and appropriate way for that conversation to take
place is between a patient and therapist.

Life

Sometimes, life is good.
And sometimes, it's bad.
Sometimes, life can even seem cruel.
But it can also be special.
Like when you become a mom or dad.
Now that we've talked about what life is sometimes,
Let's talk about what it is all the time.
When it comes down to it, Life is life.

About this poem

Life is bad and good and special and precious and so
many other adjectives. But at the end of it all, life is life. It's
not one thing or another.

Life on the spectrum

Every day, I get out of bed
And wait for work so I can stay out of my head.
For 8 to 9 hours a day, I talk to people I barely know.
But it's a big relief because I'm not the star of the show.
When you live life on the autism spectrum,
The mind can be a scary place.
You question every decision you make,
And just talking to people can make your heart race.
It can make you feel alone. Frustrated. Sad.
But it's not all bad.
People on the spectrum see the world
In a way most could never understand.
It's beautiful. And we want you to experience it.
That's why when we trust you, we reach out for your hand.
We want to connect. But it takes a while to learn how.
If you can be patient, when we're ready,
we'll show you the world in a different way.
I promise it will make you say "wow."

About this poem

I've talked a lot about vulnerability in this book. In the last
book, I told you my story in the poem out of the darkness
into the light. This is my other story. I have Asperger's
syndrome, which is a high functioning form of autism.

That's why I wanted to share this piece with you so you
can have a better understanding of what's going on in our
heads. It's important to note, however, that autism in
general is incredibly different for every person.

Listen

You could know everything,
But that won't mean anything if you don't start listening.
Listening to yourself. To your body.
To your friends and family.
Listening to the people who ask for information.
Because they won't be interested in what you have to say
If you don't care about what they have to say.

About this poem

One of the greatest things you can master is the art of
listening. And one of the most rewarding things is being
knowledgeable and being able to help people when they
ask for it.

But you need to balance the two if you want to share it.

Looking within

It's time to let myself go.
It's time to give up.
It's time to let everyone know
That I finally believe that I'm worthy of love. Praise.
That I'm finally comfortable in my own skin.
And if I can feel that way about myself,
I have faith you can too.
It all starts by looking within.

About this poem

It took years for me to be able to share my poetry with
more than just one person. And even once I did, it was still
hard for me to be able to accept that someone was being
serious when they told me they loved my work.

I know it's not an uncommon struggle, so this poem is for
all of you struggling to accept compliments and praise.
Believe that you are talented. Believe that you are
beautiful. Believe that you are enough.

Make them feel beautiful

Have you ever watched someone
look at themselves in the mirror?
It's heartbreaking.
They never see what you see.
But that's why it's important for you to be there.
To make them feel beautiful.
To Make them feel like someone cares.

About this poem

People will always see themselves differently than how the
rest of the world sees them. They may not see themselves
as attractive or beautiful. But that's why it's important for
you to be there for them. When they ask you how you they
look, take it seriously. Your answer can really make a
difference to them.

Memorial Day

Today I stand beside you to honor those we love.
The ones who made it home, the ones still fighting,
 And the ones called to guide us from above.
Today, when they sing the national anthem,
Don't be surprised if you see me cry.
It represents everything that makes me proud to be
Semper fi.
Today, it doesn't matter where you come from.
If you're here, you're American at the core.
Today, we celebrate everything we're fighting for.
Today, we'll visit our parents, daughters and sons
And tell them their war is over.
"You can finally rest in peace. It's okay.
Lay down your guns."
Whether you're a soldier, seal or marine,
Thank you for shielding us from all the things you see
That should never be seen.

About this poem

My father and grandfather are marines. I have a close
friend in the navy, and another one currently in the
marines. But I could never connect to the holiday. So, one
year, I decided to think about why it would be special to
them. What it means to them. This poem is for you.

Money for baby things (take me back)

Remember when we were kids? You asked
"Boy, what you want to do with the rest of your life?"
I said "have a couple kids with you as my wife."
Then, you started laughing.
Said "that ain't never going to happen."
Ten years later, now we both have rings.
Have the house and money for baby things.
Getting ready to be parents for the first time.
I say "I know right now, things are going our way.
But baby, if I ever lose my way,
Will you take me back to my first broken heart?"
Take me back to when I didn't know where to start.
Take me back to the country roads.
Take me back to the town where no one goes.
If I ever fall too far off the track,
Baby, take me back.

About this poem

The actual title is take me back, but after I finished writing,
I realized I put in a poem that was in my previous book.
When I was looking for other poems, I found this one. But
to keep it alphabetical, I needed to change it.

This poem was intended to be a song, and it's about not
forgetting who you are when life gets stressful, as it does
when you become parents.

More than just faith, trust, and pixie dust

Love is more than just faith, trust, and pixie dust.
It's also stress, responsibility, and lust.
But that doesn't make it any less worth fighting for.
Everything has negatives.
And sometimes, it can be hard to focus on the positive.
But no one knows what the future has in store.
So if you take it day by day,
And don't forget to have fun along the way,
Your love will grow. And who knows.
It could eventually lead to something more.

About this poem

Everything causes stress, and for a relationship to work well, there needs to be a level of responsibility, including in love. But it's one of the most rewarding things there is. This poem reminds that there are sacrifices and work must be put in for love to be successful.

My way

You say the cost of living keeps rising
So people keep dying.
If that's true, then why should we bother trying?
Growing up in small town USA,
The only opportunities for work are dangerous
And offer little pay.
If you don't have thick skin,
You won't be able to make it through the day.
I need you to say that you believe I have a choice.
That you think people will listen to what I have to say
If I raise my voice.
I don't want to leave, but I know I can't stay.
If I want a chance to live, I'll need to live life my way.

About this poem

The first line of this poem was inspired by a line from the movie In Time. Fascinating movie if you haven't seen it. From there, I wrote about how I feel it's like living in a small town. Not saying there aren't great things about it, but you really do have to have thick skin in an area where most of the jobs revolve around roofing, landscaping, and construction unless you go farther out.

I also wrote it at a time when I thought I was going to be a film critic, which is why I thought I would need to move out to California. This poem is about what it's like living in a small town and thinking about whether you're willing to take the risks necessary to live the life you want to live.

Natural disasters

Anger. Anxiety. Depression. Fear.
Imagine these feelings are a natural disaster.
What would they be?
Would they be an earthquake?
Making it feel hard to stay upright?
Do they create rifts that drive you apart from loved ones?
Are they a tsunami?
Building up until one day, they burst, drowning you?
Or are they a tornado?
Just destroying everything in its path?
If you can find a way to explain what it feels like
When you're afraid, angry, anxious, or depressed,
It can be a good start to managing it.

About this poem

Feelings like anger, anxiety, depression, and fear can be
isolating, scary, and do a lot of emotional damage. So,
when I tried to think about a metaphor, I thought of natural
disasters. This poem reminds that if you talk to someone
you trust about it, you can manage these feelings and
make them less destructive.

Never too late

I didn't tell you I loved you
Because I thought that you already knew.
I never told you you meant the world to me
Because I thought it was clear to see.
Or maybe that's just the way I wanted it to be.
But now that you've gone away,
I asked myself if it's too late to tell you these things.
A voice answered back "It's never too late."

About this poem

We can't take back words we've said and things we've
done. So it makes sense that people would think it's too
late; the damage has been done. But it's not meaningless
to apologize or explain what came out wrong. Even if it
doesn't change anything, it's a matter of respect and doing
the right thing.

New skin

Today is ending so tomorrow can begin.
Tonight, your eyes will rest as you grow your new skin.
This is something our body does every night
So we can have the best chance
To keep fighting the good fight.
In the morning, you might not feel the best.
So make sure you have enough energy to take on the day
By eating breakfast.
Your body will do whatever it takes
To make sure you survive.
But it's up to you to take care of your new skin
So you can thrive.

About this poem

When you sleep, the body repairs itself and hormones
change it, like making hair longer or making kids grow
taller. New skin is about accepting these new changes as
they happen and taking care of yourself.

Night doesn't last forever

You can't see the light because you are the light.
So, don't worry about your scars.
They'll heal as you fly across the sky like a shooting star.
Don't forget the night doesn't last forever.
Even in the land of the midnight sun.
As long as you show up, half the battle has been won.

About this poem

This is a poem about how, even if we don't have any hope,
even if we're going through rough times, good things will
happen eventually. You just have to keep showing up.

No one, everyone, anyone, someone

NO ONE can help or please EVERYONE.
But ANYONE can help or please SOMEONE.

About this poem

Yup. It's true. Not that pleasing anyone is important, but it makes us feel good. This poem is what's called a couplet; a two line poem.

Not alone

"What would you do for loved ones?"
"Anything."
"What would you do for yourself?"
"Nothing."
"Why not?"
"It's selfish."
"Why is it selfish?"
"Because I'm okay being alone. They're not."
"First, just because you're okay being alone
Doesn't mean you should be.
And second, you're not alone.
You have me."

About this poem

Honestly, I'm not sure who is having this conversation. But
the sentiment remains. This poem serves as a reminder
that even if you feel alone, there's always someone to be
there for you. And while it's great to want to support other
people, there's nothing wrong for doing things for yourself.
After all, this is YOUR life.

Not the end

It's not the end of the world.
It's not even the end of the day.
Just because the sky is gray
Doesn't mean the sun can't come out
As if to say, "it's okay."
Remember. Most of us see the world in color.
If you don't like the ones you see,
Just close your eyes and breathe.
Please don't give up, and I promise you'll see
It's not the end.

About this poem

Another poem to inspire you to keep going.

Not your job

It's not your job to prove them wrong.
Sometimes, just walking away
Says more than words ever could.
It's not your job to fight in a fight that's not yours.
But sometimes, it's what's right.
It's not your job to forgive someone or take them back.
Listen to your heart, you will be on the right track.
Your only job is to be yourself.
To do what's best for you, your health, your happiness.

About this poem

Just like the world doesn't owe you anything, you don't
owe the world anything either. You may want your job to
be taking care of everyone else and practicing forgiveness.
But your first job is to take care of yourself and your
happiness.

Once upon a time

"I wish I wasn't so different from everyone."
"You've got more in common with people than you think."
"Oh yeah? Like what?"
"Well, once upon a time, we were smaller.
Then, we grew taller. Or rounder.
Maybe more than we'd like, but we all grew stronger."
"Well, I don't feel very strong right now."
"And that's okay. We all fall.
Sometimes like a sack of bricks.
Sometimes with the grace of a sunset.
But at some point, we all get up.
And when you're ready to stand,
 I think you'll find there's fight left in you yet."

About this poem

It's easy to feel alone. Ostracized. Like you have nothing in common with anyone. But for all the things that make us feel disconnected, there are still things that connect all of us. This poem reminds us that we're not as different from each other as we think we are, and we're stronger than we realize.

One more

If we had just one more hour,
One more day,
Could we find another way?
Could we find the words to say
What we've always wanted to say?
Could we find a reason to stay?
And yes. It's true that one more hour, one more day
Could make things worse.
But isn't it worth the risk if you can find value?
Worth?

About this poem

It only takes a second to change things. Imagine what
could happen with another hour. Another day. Some days
are worse than others. And it may seem like all hope is
gone. But you never know what could happen the next
day. It might be the day you have a chance to escape. It
might be the day you have a chance to heal. Or maybe,
just maybe, the next day might be the one where you're
heard. Validated. Isn't that a chance worth taking?

One-way ticket

Dreaming about the future
While living in the past
Is a one-way ticket to madness.

About this poem

if you reject current ideals and ways of life, but you dream
about the future, it will drive you crazy because it will never
happen.

Only time will tell

Only time will tell how far you've come.
Only time will tell how far you'll go.
Only time will tell how much you've learned.
Only time will tell how much you've grown.
Only time will tell how much you've lived.
Only time will tell when you'll die.
But since we don't know what time will say,
Let's try to make the most of every day.

About this poem

Time tells all. But we don't know what time will say.
Another carpe diem poem.

Protect yourself

The hardest lesson to learn
Is that hiding your feelings protects no one.
The hardest thing to accept
Is that you don't need to protect anyone.

About this poem

In my personal experience, people are passive aggressive
because they are afraid if they say how they really feel to
someone's face, it will make someone upset and be
awkward. But talking about them behind their back isn't
any better.

As for the second part, people can take care of themselves
for the most part. The only one you really need to protect is
yourself. Think about it this way. You can't protect anyone
if you don't protect yourself.

Questions and answers

"Who cares?"
"I care."
"Why?"
"Because I've been there. And I know how much it means
to be able to have someone to talk to
When life gets so unfair."
"You have no idea what I'm going through.
How dare you say you understand."
"You're right. I very well might not understand.
But I'm willing to listen.
And when you're finished, if you want,
I'll help however I can."

About this poem

In this poem, a person is going through a rough time. They
feel no one cares about them. They're suspicious when
someone says they do. The person is defensive when the
person trying to help them says they understand.

This poem suggests that just offering to listen to someone
can be a big help. It can make them feel heard.

Rainbow within you

Sometimes, I feel blue.
Sometimes, I see red.
Sometimes, I smell orange
Or eat yellow bananas when I get out of bed.
Sometimes, I'm green with envy.
I'm sure there's indigo and violet
Somewhere in there, too.
But just because the only color you see
Is the color of your skin,
It doesn't mean there isn't a rainbow within you.

About this poem

Colorful. That's the word we use to describe someone's personality. And there's so many colors. Unfortunately, sometimes it's hard to see. This poem reminds you that sometimes, there's more to people than meets the eye.

Real

In case you didn't know, the pain you feel,
The fears you have, the love you give, Is real.

About this poem

Sometimes, bullies or trolls can make us feel that what we
feel doesn't matter. It isn't real. This poem assures you it
is. That it's not just in your head. And if you feel something
is wrong, physically or mentally, don't be afraid to get a
second opinion.

Reflections from our imperfections

You hate the gray in your hair.
I hate my weight.
You hate your freckles.
I hate my dimples.
We both hate when we get pimples.
You don't understand why people love your nose.
But that's the way it goes.
These things embarrass us.
But honestly, they're the best parts.
Because we find proof that we're human in the reflection
Given off by these things we call imperfections

About this poem

One of the silent, unpopular truths is that there is no such
thing as perfect. That's why we call things like pimples or
weird shaped noses imperfections. They may be annoying,
but they're not really anything to be ashamed of or
embarrassed about. They can happen to anyone.

Roar

Every day, you make a choice
To stay silent or raise your voice.
And that's your choice, and I respect it.
I just want you to know that if today,
You decide you want to be a lion
And let people hear you roar,
I'll roar with you
Until you don't feel alone or broken anymore.

About this poem

Everyone has a choice. Multiple choices. You can speak
up for someone. You can speak up for yourself. You can
run away. You can choose to say nothing. But if you have
something to say, and you decide to say it, someone will
respect it and support you for it.

Room

There's room to live.
There's room to love.
There's room to hate.
There's room to forgive.
There's room to change.
There's room to grow.
There's room to breathe.
There's room to believe.
There's room to grieve.
There's room to run.
There's room to have fun.
There's room for everything and everyone.
You just have to make room for it.

About this poem

This poem is about realizing there is room for everyone
and every feeling.

Say it

Don't let yourself be swept away
By the promise of another day.
And if you have something to say, say it.
Because no one knows exactly how long we get to stay.

About this poem

Another carpe diem poem. This poem encourages you to
say what's on your mind because you never know how
long you have.

Second chances

Second chances are pots of gold at the end of a rainbow.
But we treat them like a prize from a box of cracker jacks;
Cherished one minute, then the next we put it back.
Not taking things for granted is easier said than done.
But if you get a second chance,
Treat it like it's the only one.

About this poem

Not that most people don't deserve second chances, but
this poem asks that if you're given one, take it seriously.

See you at the end

When will you give your heart a chance to soar?
What's it going to take for you to believe
You deserve more?
I know this is a theme I've explored before.
That when people push you down,
You don't have to stay on the floor.
But you still don't believe me.
So I'll keep saying it until you feel it in your core.
You are not a product of your environment.
You can change the score.
The first step is to find happiness.
Then, it's time to start opening doors.
It'll take some time. So make sure to bring a friend.
Don't give up. I'll see you at the end.

About this poem

See you at the end is about not believing in yourself,
standing up for yourself, and then when you're ready to be
happy and healthy, you accept help from friends when you
need it, and you don't stop until you're happy.

Stick together

Once again, everything has changed.
This time, it was for the worst.
But we'll be okay.
Because we've always thought it was more important
To help an injured runner than finishing first.
We do this because in the end,
It doesn't matter who finishes first or last.
As long as we stick together,
No matter what we face, we can kick its ass.

About this poem

Stick together is about how much easier it is to get through
a difficult time if everyone works together to solve the
problem and support each other.

Still a good day

I'm here. You're here. It's a good day.
Nice idea, right?
But it doesn't always work that way.
Sometimes, the skies are gray.
And you don't have the energy to find words to say.
Some days, people die, and you can't help but feel
Betrayed.
But you know what? We're still here. We still remember.
So it's still a good day.

About this poem

Still a good day is a poem to comfort those who have lost
someone recently. Your life may seem empty, and it
doesn't feel like a good day. But as long as you can carry
on their memory, they're still a part of you. As long as
you're alive, it's still a good day.

Stuck in the middle

This is not the end.
It's not the beginning.
It's not even the beginning of the end.
Sorry to say, but you're stuck in the middle.
But the middle's not a bad place to be.
You learn what you didn't know in the beginning,
And you find the skills you need to get to the end.
It's where you learn from your mistakes
And meet your friends.
The ones who make everything worth it.
So don't feel stuck.
And don't be so anxious to get to the end.
You never know. It might suck.

About this poem

People always talk about how they hate being the middle
child or caught in the middle of a situation. This poem
explains why the middle might not be such a bad place.

Support

Physical death is permanent.
But emotional death, (numbness, depression) is a starfish.
It can grow back through a process called support.

About this poem

Have you ever been so depressed, so mentally exhausted
to the point you say, "I feel dead inside"? This poem was
written to inspire hope that you can feel better when you
have people who support you and make you believe there
can still be good times.

Tell me

Don't be afraid to tell me I'm wrong.
Because I won't learn anything if you tell me I'm right.
Don't be afraid to tell me the truth.
I promise it will never start a fight.

About this poem

As I said earlier, in my experience, people are afraid to say
what's on their mind for fear it will make someone upset or
make the situation uncomfortable. This poem explains why
it's better to tell someone when they are wrong.

Tell your story

Even when you're going through hell,
Even when you think you've found the bottom of the well,
You still have a story to tell.
And in a world of seven billion people,
Someone's bound to listen
Whether or not you're under a steeple.
And while you're at it, that's the best time
To chase your dreams.
Because you don't have much to lose
When you feel you lost yourself years ago.

About this poem

Tell your story is about not holding anything back when
you're going through a rough time. It might feel
embarrassing or like you're burdening someone by saying
what's going on under the surface, but it can make people
understand you better. And if you accept it, it can help
them figure out how to help you more effectively.

That's what it's all about

It's not about me. It's not about you.
It's about what we do.
What we do with the time we have left.
With the people we meet.
With the challenges we face.
With the rumors we hear.
When we come face to face with our fears.
With the love we have.
With the love we lose.
What we do when we have to choose.
What we do when we realize we have responsibilities.
That's what life's all about to me.

About this poem

Life is full of choices. This poem is about recognizing that
it's the choices we make that are important.

The games of life and love

Tonight, I'm going to leave everything on the line.
Tonight, I'll be alone again, or you'll be mine.
Tonight, I'm facing all my fears.
Regret, loneliness, denial, shame.
But that's what you have to risk
If you want to play the games of life and love.

About this poem

I wrote this poem when I thought about why I would want
to try to fall in love again after having my heart broken. I
realized you have to take risks to be able to have a fulfilling
life and a true love.

The more you know

It pays to stay informed.
But you have to pay to stay informed.
Because the more you know, the more you grow.

About this poem

Regardless of what you do in life, whether it be politics,
being a celebrity, even being a garbageman, if you aren't
informed on what's going on in the world, if you don't keep
learning about new things, it is very difficult to keep a job
let alone a conversation.

That's why they say college is an investment. Even the
newspaper, or the blog you read online is an investment.
This poem reminds the importance of school and reading.

These days

These days, the years come slow and go by so fast.
These days, it's hard to make memories
And even harder to make them last.
These days, we're afraid of ourselves
As much as we are of strangers.
These days, we see everything as a danger.
These days, we're getting farther apart
Even though we're starving for connection.
But the isolation is a great opportunity for self-reflection.
Unfortunately, we look at the clock
And think we need to rush.
These days, we don't take enough time
To appreciate the power of a kiss, hug, or touch.
These days, words have more power than ever.
So please take the time to think about what you say.
It may change how people think of you
For the rest of your days.

About this poem

These days, it seems like we're more afraid. Like we don't
have time to slow down. This poem is about the
importance of making the time to slow down and think
about the consequences of our actions and words.

Things change

They say things change.
And that's absolutely true.
Money. Entertainment.
Clothes and shoes.
But the thing is, none of that matters
Unless people change.
The same people are still screaming,
Still fighting for the same reasons.
We've built a world where words
Have as much power as angels and demons.
I'll be the first to admit. I have no idea where to start.
But we need to change now
Before we drift even further apart.

About this poem

Change is inevitable. And yet, we still struggle to prevent it.
This poem is about actively causing change in ourselves
and our communities to come together.

Time of your life

Time heals.
Time bends.
Time gives us chances to make amends.
Time gives.
Time takes.
In time, we learn from our mistakes.
For a time you'll live.
In time, you'll die.
So make the most of your time.
Don't be afraid to reach for the sky.

About this poem

Another poem about making the most of your day. Of your life. Because we don't know how much time we have.

To be happy

"If you'd be with me,
I'd give you the world."
"I don't want the world."
"Why not?"
"The world today Is different than it was yesterday.
It's different from the world we'll live in tomorrow.
I might not want the world tomorrow."
"So what do you want?"
"To be happy."

About this poem

People tend to make promises they can't keep to get what
they want. When someone is pursuing a relationship, it's
not uncommon for someone to offer the world; anything
they want if they would be willing to be in a relationship
with them. This poem is about realizing that sometimes,
people just want simple things. They aren't impressed or
inspired by material things. They want emotional
connection.

To change or not to change

Just because the world changes
Every day, hour, minute, and second,
Doesn't mean you have to.
But, then again, maybe that's exactly why you should.

About this poem

Food for thought.

Truth

"the" truth is not "the" truth.
It's your truth.
Some people will subscribe to your truth.
Others will shun it.
But it's yours.
And no one can take that from you.
So own it.

About this poem

With the exception of a few universal truths, the truth is a
matter of interpretation. It's a belief.

Wanted

If you know you're wanted,
Please don't take that for granted.
Because someone you know doesn't know.
Doesn't believe.
They've had peers tell them things like
"You're a burden,
Or "you'll never go anywhere" so much,
They start to believe it.
If you're reading this, and you're feeling this way,
Let me be the first to say: "I want you."
I want you to live.
I want you to not be afraid to love.
I want you to find courage. And pride.
I want you to rise above.
Because I've been there.
And you deserve to feel wanted.

About this poem

Just like saying something positive enough can make you
feel better, having someone tell you something negative
can have just as much an effect.

This poem is about helping you realize someone does
appreciate you being in their life even if you don't know.

War and peace

We live in war but die in peace.
Doesn't matter if your face is full of wrinkles
Or caked in grease.
We live in war with ourselves.
With emotions and strangers.
With finding hope when every corner you turn,
You only find a new danger.
But death is proof that war can end.
So don't give up.
Stay strong; and know that you won't break if you bend.

About this poem

This poem is about equality. We all struggle with things.
But we can also overcome them.

We're all different

You can call me names and make me fall.
But you don't know what I can do
When my back's against the wall.
You can mock me and tell me I look like a freak.
But it's okay because these things don't make me weak.
We're all different.
So why are we so afraid of how people look, talk, or think?
We're all different. So let's embrace it and have a drink.

About this poem

We're so desperate to be different from everyone else, but
we're terrified of the people who truly are different from
everyone else. This poem is about embracing and
respecting each other's differences rather than fearing it.

What do you have to lose?

Life's not going to wait for you.
So, tell me, what are you waiting for?
If you want to chase your dreams,
Pick yourself up off the floor.
The frustration and fear bringing tears to your eyes
Will give you the strength to get what you want.
Just keep your eyes on the prize.
We've all got things we want to do
But let our heads fill with doubt.
The trick is to listen to your heart
And drown all the other voices out.
What you do with your time
Is something only you can choose.
But even if you fail, tell me, what do you have to lose?

About this poem

This poem is about not letting fear of failure stop you from living the life you want to live. If you fail, you can learn what you did wrong so next time, you have a better chance to succeed.

You've got a shot

Don't worry about where you'll go in life
Or how much you'll do.
You don't need that much pressure.
You're barely 22!
But if you are, it's okay.
Because I know you'll go far.
The key is to go with the flow for as long as you can.
But some day you'll fall in more ways than one.
But you'll always get up
Because there's more work to be done.
But just because there's more work
Doesn't mean there's any less fun.
Sometimes, though, it may be hard to find.
Somedays, all you'll want to do is run.
You won't care where.
You'll just want to go away.
But away can be a scary place.
A place with no rules.
Of course, that's exactly why some decide to stay.
Whatever you decide, it's your decision to make.
And don't be embarrassed when you make a mistake.
Because you don't know what you don't know.
And at first, you won't know a lot.
But you'll get there.
At least, I think you have a shot.

About this poem

Inspired by Dr. Seuss's Oh! The places you'll go.

Congratulations! You made it to the end of my second book. Thank you for sticking around this long. So, here's a bonus poem called not a mistake.

Trying to get ahead, but I can't silence all these thoughts
Inside of my head.
Looking everywhere for a place to reset; get a grip.
But my demons are screaming so loud,
It's like I'm on a bad trip.
They say god never gives us more than we can take.
But I don't know how much longer I can hold my breath
Before I find myself at the bottom of the lake.
I clutch my chest gasping for air.
And with my hand on my heart, I pray for a new day.
A chance to prove I deserve a new start.
I close my eyes one last time and let myself go.
The demons leave my mind, body, and soul.
I feel a rush come over and open my eyes
To realize it was all a dream; I'm still alive.
Now that I made it through, my mission is clear.
I know what to do.
I'll use my experiences to help the broken and scarred
Find their faith.
And help them believe loving, living, fighting, is not a mistake.

About this poem

When I was younger, I felt ostracized by my peers and felt alone. Even though I knew I had my family and close friends. At the same time, I was also bullied to the point where I started telling myself things that they would say so that I believed it, hoping it would hurt less when they brought it up. As my mental health deteriorated, I got to the point where I didn't want to go on. But then I fell in love. I had someone accept me for who I was and made me realize I was enough. This poem is about what it felt like to reach my breaking point, and why I write poetry. I don't want anyone else to feel like I did.

Made in United States
North Haven, CT
03 January 2022

13932704R00065